HOW TO
✶ DRAW ✶

THE WORLD OF
JACQUELINE WILSON

www.randomhousechildrens.co.uk

NICK SHARRATT has written and illustrated many books for children and won numerous awards for his picture books, including the Children's Book Award and the Educational Writers' Award. He has also enjoyed great success illustrating Jacqueline Wilson's books. Nick lives in Edinburgh.

JACQUELINE WILSON is an extremely well-known and hugely popular author who served as Children's Laureate from 2005–7. She has been awarded a number of prestigious awards, including the British Children's Book of the Year and the Guardian Children's Fiction Award, the Smarties Prize and the Children's Book Award. In 2002 Jacqueline was given an OBE for services to literacy in schools and in 2008 she was appointed a Dame. She was the author most borrowed from British libraries in the last decade.

ALSO AVAILABLE BY NICK SHARRATT

SHARK IN THE PARK
SHARK IN THE DARK
SHARK IN THE PARK ON A WINDY DAY

WITH
PIPPA GOODHART
YOU CHOOSE
JUST IMAGINE

WITH
KES GRAY
EAT YOUR PEAS
REALLY REALLY
YOU DO!
YUK!
006 AND A BIT
A BUNCH OF DAISIES
TIGER WAYS
ACCIDENTALLY ON PURPOSE
SUPER DAISY AND THE PERIL OF PLANET PEA

WITH
ELIZABETH LINDSAY
SOCKS

WITH
GILES ANDREAE
PANTS
MORE PANTS

WRITTEN BY JACQUELINE WILSON
AND ILLUSTRATED BY NICK SHARRATT

WHERE TO START
THE DINOSAUR'S PACKED LUNCH
THE MONSTER STORY-TELLER

FOR YOUNGER
READERS
BURIED ALIVE!
CLIFFHANGER
GLUBBSLYME
LIZZIE ZIPMOUTH
SLEEPOVERS
THE CAT MUMMY
THE MUM-MINDER
THE WORRY WEBSITE

FIRST CLASS
FRIENDS
BAD GIRLS
BEST FRIENDS
SECRETS
VICKY ANGEL

HISTORICAL
ADVENTURES
OPAL PLUMSTEAD
QUEENIE
THE LOTTIE PROJECT

ALL ABOUT
JACQUELINE WILSON
JACKY DAYDREAM
MY SECRET DIARY

FAMILY DRAMAS
CANDYFLOSS
CLEAN BREAK
COOKIE
FOUR CHILDREN AND IT
LILY ALONE
LITTLE DARLINGS
LOLA ROSE
MIDNIGHT
THE BED AND BREAKFAST STAR
THE ILLUSTRATED MUM
THE LONGEST WHALE SONG
THE SUITCASE KID
KATY

MOST POPULAR CHARACTERS
HETTY FEATHER
SAPPHIRE BATTERSEA
EMERALD STAR
DIAMOND
THE STORY OF TRACY BEAKER
THE DARE GAME
STARRING TRACY BEAKER

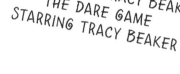

STORIES ABOUT SISTERS
DOUBLE ACT
THE BUTTERFLY CLUB
THE DIAMOND GIRLS
THE WORST THING
ABOUT MY SISTER

FOR OLDER READERS

DUSTBIN BABY
GIRLS IN LOVE
GIRLS IN TEARS
GIRLS OUT LATE
GIRLS UNDER PRESSURE
KISS
LOVE LESSONS
MY SISTER JODIE

ALSO AVAILABLE
PAWS AND WHISKERS
THE JACQUELINE WILSON
CHRISTMAS CRACKER
JACQUELINE WILSON'S HAPPY HOLIDAYS
THE JACQUELINE WILSON TREASURY

HOW TO DRAW
A DOUBLEDAY BOOK 978 0 857 53489 7

Published in Great Britain by Doubleday,
an imprint of Random House Children's Publishers UK
A Penguin Random House Company

This edition published 2015

1 3 5 7 9 10 8 6 4 2

Penguin Random House is committed to a sustainable future
for our business, our readers and our planet. This book is made from
Forest Stewardship Council® certified paper.

MIX
Paper from
responsible sources
FSC® C018179

Set in Pencil Pete and Oklahoma

Random House Children's Publishers UK,
61–63 Uxbridge Road, London W5 5SA

www.randomhousechildrens.co.uk
www.totallyrandombooks.co.uk
www.randomhouse.co.uk

Addresses for companies within The Random House Group Limited
can be found at: www.randomhouse.co.uk/offices.htm

THE RANDOM HOUSE GROUP Limited Reg. No. 954009

A CIP catalogue record for this book is available from the British Library.

Printed in China

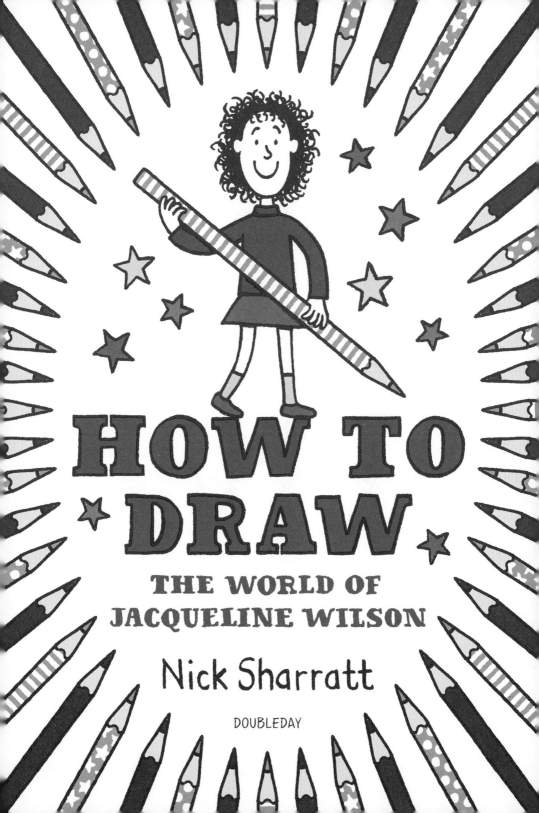

HOW TO

★ DRAW ★

THE WORLD OF
JACQUELINE WILSON

Nick Sharratt

DOUBLEDAY

FOR KINGSWELLS SCHOOL

CONTENTS

INTRODUCTION FROM NICK SHARRATT

I **GUESS I'VE** loved drawing from the very first time I held a crayon in my hand and had a go at making scribbles on a sheet of paper. I can't actually remember that far back (it was a very long time ago!) but I do know that by the time I was in the Infants, it was my number one favourite thing to do. There is a photograph of me aged six, sitting in the back garden, busily producing pictures and looking blissfully happy. In that photo, I'm painting, but it didn't matter if I was using paint or pencils or wax crayons or felt tips – as long as I was creating images, I was content.

I don't know where my enthusiasm for art came from. Unlike other illustrators I know, I'm not from an artistic background and I don't think I've ever seen my mum or dad draw a single thing in their lives – but they could tell how much it mattered to me, and always gave me plenty of encouragement, as well as lots of paper and lovely drawing materials to experiment with.

When I was at primary school, art was far and away the lesson I liked best. I was soon given the role of 'artist' in the class, so that if a school poster needed to be made, or a class display required some fancy lettering, I would be the one picked to do it. When I was eight, I somehow ended up creating a huge Christmas mural for the school hall all by myself. It involved drawing almost life-sized pictures of carol singers and making stained glass windows from colour tissue paper, and it was a huge amount of work – but I loved doing it.

In Year Five, my class was planning an assembly on hobbies and over the weekend I drew a large picture of a market square with my felt tip pens.

I inked in stripy stalls and interesting-looking characters out shopping, and I put in loads of detail. I drew a stall selling fruit, vegetables and sweets, one selling toys and one selling fashionable jewellery (Jacqueline would have approved!). I took my drawing into school for the assembly and I can still remember the thrilling feeling I got when my teacher decided it should be pinned up in the hall so that everyone could enjoy looking at it. That was when I decided I wanted to be an artist when I grew up.

When I left school I got a place at art college, like most of my illustrator friends. On my course, as well as working on my drawing, I learned a bit about design and typography, which are useful things for an illustrator to have some knowledge about.

After that, I began my life as a professional artist, drawing pictures for magazines, newspapers, advertising, packaging and children's books. The book work was the most fun, a world where I could really be inventive and stretch my imagination, exploring all kinds of fantastic subjects and bringing to life great characters created by the writers I worked with. So that was the kind of illustration I decided to concentrate on.

I was extremely excited when I was asked to illustrate *The Story of Tracy Beaker*. It was my first children's novel and I was a bit nervous, but Jacqueline is such a wonderful, descriptive writer that, having read the manuscript, I could see quite clearly in my head how Tracy should look and visualize the world around her easily. I will let you in on a secret, though – I didn't read the story quite closely enough, and it was only when I'd done all the artwork that I realized I'd given Tracy a funny little skirt

INTRODUCTION FROM NICK SHARRATT

when the text actually mentioned jeans. But because Jacqueline is the kind, sweet person she is, she said it was easier for her to alter the words than for me to change all the pictures. Not all authors would have been so understanding!

Many, many books later, Jacqueline and I have been working together for more than two decades. I'm so lucky to have been given scores of vivid, memorable characters to create images for. Jacky's words completely bring them to life on the page, and by the time I've done my bit and finished my set of illustrations, they feel like real friends. Tracy, Hetty, Biscuits, the *Sleepover* girls, Ruby and Garnet, Floss, Queenie the cat . . . It's a very long list, and I've enjoyed drawing them all.

In this book I'll be giving you my tips on easy ways to draw Jacqueline's amazing characters for yourself. In addition, a certain curly-haired girl will be putting on all kinds of outfits and taking you to places and showing you things that are great fun to draw too. Sharpen those pencils and happy drawing!

Nick Sharratt

INTRODUCTION FROM JACQUELINE WILSON

DO YOU LIKE reading my books? I wonder which is your favourite. Perhaps you like *The Story of Tracy Beaker* or *Hetty Feather* or *Sleepovers*? Say your favourite title out loud and think hard about the book. Have you conjured up in your head an image of a girl with wild black curls and a cheeky expression? A pale girl with bright red hair and a strange uncomfortable uniform? A girl with plaits tucked up in a big bed with three friends and one deadly enemy? You've just visualized Nick's brilliant covers. Think of *any* Jacqueline Wilson book written over the past twenty-five years and you'll see it through Nick's eyes. He brings all my characters to life on the page – and how grateful I am to him!

I know from all the lovely illustrated letters you send me that you love Nick's artwork too, and nearly always copy your favourite characters at the top of the page. You're going to find *this* book the biggest treat ever, because Nick has shared all his artistic secrets and shows us how to draw exactly like him. I've copied Nick's artwork over the years to make my own letters to fans more interesting, but I've never managed to make my drawings more than passable. But now I'm going to keep *How to Draw* on my desk and follow Nick's tips and hopefully improve considerably. I'll never be a true creative artist, of course – but it will be such fun copying!

I'm so lucky to have had such a long and happy artistic partnership with Nick. He works with other writers too, and he produces many delightful picture books of his own – but I'm so glad that we also always collaborate on two books a year.

I had several skilled illustrators before I got teamed up with Nick, but I don't think it's coincidence that my books really started selling splendidly when they had Nick's colourful covers and detailed black and white illustrations illuminating the text. Nick makes his artwork come alive. It's magical watching him draw, seeing how with a few deft black lines he can create a real character who looks happy, sad, anxious, angry . . .

We first worked together when I wrote *The Story of Tracy Beaker*. I knew I wanted lots of pictures throughout the book, as if Tracy herself had drawn them all. I knew it would enliven each page and encourage reluctant readers to work their way happily through the whole book. My then editor, David Fickling, said he thought he knew the very chap to do the illustrations and suggested that Nick and I meet up. We were both quite shy with each other at first. Nick was wearing an unusually formal suit and though I liked him enormously right from the start, I did wonder if he was quirky and outrageous enough to express my bizarre Miss Beaker. Then I bent down to get a hankie out of my handbag and glimpsed an inch of Nick's sock between his trouser hem and his shoe. It was a brilliant canary yellow! I knew then that Nick was the perfect choice.

Lots of you write to say that you're my number one fan.

Well, I want it down on record that I'm *Nick's* number one fan. It's so exciting when I send him a new story, waiting to see how he'll visualize the characters. He's always spot on, knowing exactly how they should look. I love his clear black lines – his artwork is a joy to colour in. I love the way everything is balanced on the page, giving a deep sense of satisfaction. I love the telling detail, the little witty jokes, the sheer fun and delight in every picture.

I treasure Nick's artwork – indeed, I have a whole wall in my living room hung with his illustrations, many of them special presents to me. I also treasure Nick himself. I'm so happy that we've become great friends as well as artistic partners.

We don't get to see each other as often as we'd like, as I live near London and Nick now lives in Edinburgh, but it's a big treat whenever we do. We also try to go on little country holidays together where we eat a lot, laugh a lot, do some sight-seeing and go on long walks. There's only one rule on these holidays: I don't do any writing at all and Nick doesn't draw.

Thank goodness Nick draws every day when he's *not* on holiday. This fantastic book is *your* chance to develop your own artistic talent. Have fun!

Jacqueline Wilson

GETTING STARTED

THIS BOOK WILL show you how I like to draw characters, animals, places and objects – but I'm not saying that you absolutely must draw them like me. For example, you might prefer adding more detail to your characters' eyes than I do, drawing the iris, pupil, eyelashes and eyelids and so on – so don't hesitate to do that if you want to. This isn't a drawing book with rules – well, only one: drawing should be fun!

MATERIALS

It doesn't really matter what kind of paper you have, but a drawing pad of cartridge paper gives you a really nice surface to draw on. I actually quite like working on printer paper too, and you do get loads of sheets in a pack!

Equally, you can draw with any kind of pencil or pen. For line drawing, I like using a pencil more than anything else. Have you noticed how pencils often have a letter and number on them?

They're there to tell you how hard or soft the pencil is. The ones I use are labelled **2B** and **3B**, which makes them softer than pencils with H numbers. I think they give a nicer, darker line too. If I'm doing quite a large drawing, for a cover perhaps, I will use a **6B** pencil because it's really good for drawing thicker lines.

I try to avoid rubbing out if I can, since it can roughen the paper a little, but if you have to, a line drawn with a soft rather than a hard pencil isn't too hard to erase. And the softer your rubber, the better.

Occasionally I draw in charcoal and then I use something called a putty rubber, which is so soft you can knead it between your fingers. It's really excellent for cleaning up charcoal illustrations which can get pretty messy!

Drawing with a pen is great for a really good black line that stands out clearly. There are all kinds of pens to choose from and it's basically a matter of the one that makes the line that you like best. I use a special technical pen, but a thin-nibbed felt tip or marker can work just as well. Biro can be fun to draw with, but the line can sometimes get a bit smudged when you add colour. The thing about drawing in ink is that you can't do any rubbing out, so it might be a good idea to sketch out things in very faint pencil line first.

If you do want to change something in a drawing that you've done in pen, you could do what I do, and cut out a patch of paper just big enough to hide the mistake. Glue it into place carefully, and make sure the glue is completely dry before redrawing your lines on the patch.

One more tip – when I was young, I would often find myself abandoning a drawing after I'd only just begun, because I didn't think it was quite right. Sometimes I'd end up with a whole pad full of barely-started drawings surrounded by lots of empty white paper. Try to complete your pictures if you can – it's so satisfying to achieve a finished piece of work, and even if you weren't too sure along the way, you might be in for a really nice surprise when you get to the end!

ADDING COLOUR

Once you've drawn your illustration in a black line you might want to add some colour. Over time I've used all sorts of materials to colour up my artwork: marker pens, watercolours, coloured pencils, pastels, wax crayons . . .

To begin with I filled in Jacqueline's cover illustrations with acrylic inks which come in nice bright colours, and I then added finer details with artists' wax crayons. More recently I've been scanning my line drawings into my computer and colouring them up digitally. I like the smooth, even effect I can achieve with a computer and oddly, working this way really reminds me of the fun I had colouring in with felt tip pens when I was a boy. All I ever wanted as birthday and Christmas presents were bumper packs of felt tips because I got through them so quickly,

but I loved using them because I felt more in control than with other colouring materials.

Use whatever you like to colour your drawings. If (unlike me) you're really good with paint and a paintbrush, that is fantastic. Ideally the paper you work on will be thick enough to take the paint without going bumpy because of the moisture.

You might want to use felt tips, and if you do, here are a couple of tips that I taught myself in the days when they were my favourite medium. Felt tip colours are wonderfully vibrant but they can sometimes be a bit too strong if you're colouring in sky or human skin, for example. To achieve a less intense shade with a felt tip, instead of filling an area with solid colour, you could try repeating diagonal lines like this:

Or you could stipple, drawing lots of little dots close together to create a tone like the picture on the opposite page. It takes a while, but it can be quite enjoyable if you're not in a hurry!

Alternatively, you could mix your materials and use coloured pencils for the lighter colours and felts for the stronger tones in your drawing.

One more thing you could try is colouring gently over the felt tip colour with a white pencil, although this technique requires a bit of practice.

Talking of colouring pencils, like black graphite pencils, some are softer than others and they're the ones I prefer. Why not try taking a cotton bud and gently rubbing the area you've filled in to blend the pencil marks together and get an even smoother look? It's a technique I use a lot when I give a character circles of cheek colour and I want to blur the edges a little.

Painting a very light wash of water with a fine paintbrush over both felt tip ink and coloured pencil can give you some interesting results too. It's fun to experiment with colouring techniques, but do have a bit of a practice first, before using a new method on a drawing that you really don't want to risk spoiling!

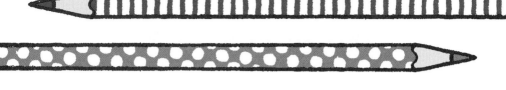

How to draw ...
FACES

LOOK AT ALL THESE faces that I've drawn in Jacqueline's books. How many do you recognize? They all have certain things in common: dots for eyes and very simple lines to make the nose and the mouth. But I hope they all look a little different to one another.

Small mouth

Pointy chin

Wide Mouth

Round face

Freckles

I try to achieve this by giving every character a unique head shape, playing with the positioning of the facial features and adding an individual haircut (though Jacqueline and I have our own favourite styles: for Jacqueline it's plaits and for me it's short hair that sticks straight up!).

Tiny nose

Thin face

Dimples

Firm jaw

Eyes close together

Bulbous nose

WHEN I DRAW a face, I start with the outline of the head and then add the eyes, nose and mouth.

The eyes should be at the
same level as the ears

Happy

Laughing

Anxious

Upset

Sad

Grumpy

To show how a character is feeling I use the eyebrows, mouth and cheeks for conveying emotions.

Cross

Furious

Hungry

Surprised

Shocked

Crafty

Cheeky

Embarrassed

Confused

WHAT THOUGHTS DO YOU think are going through the minds of these characters?

YOU CAN ALSO TELL a lot about how people are feeling by what they do with their hands.

AS WELL AS DRAWING faces from the front, you could try drawing them in profile, which means from the side.

FACES

In reality the ear wouldn't be right at the back of the head – I just like to draw it there! Do you recognize any of the passengers?

A **SILHOUETTE CAN** work very well when you draw the face in profile. A silhouette is made by drawing a dark shape against a light background, so it looks like a shadow. Begin with a simple egg-shaped head and then work up the details – a nose, a chin, hair, lips, even eyelashes and spectacles. I used lots of silhouettes in the *Hetty Feather* books.

YOU'LL SEE ALL kinds of hairstyles in this book, but an impressive number of Jacqueline's heroines have plaited hair. Tracy even has a go at plaiting hers in *The Story of Tracy Beaker*. Like tying real plaits, drawing them needs a little practice.

1. Start with a curved line.

2. Cross it with a line sloping the other way.

3. Add another curved line like the first.

4. Add another curved line like the second.

5. Repeat as many times as you want.

6. Finish your plait with a band or a bow, and a fan shape to show the loose hair at the bottom.

How to draw ...
BODIES AND ACTIONS

PEOPLE COME IN all shapes and sizes and it's great to get lots of variety in your pictures, especially if you're drawing a crowd scene.

A strong person might have broad shoulders

Glamorous ladies can be curvy!

Older people often stoop

IT'S QUITE RARE that I illustrate a person just standing still. Here are Jacqueline's characters doing all kinds of actions. Some are trickier to draw than others – turn over for a handy tip on how to sketch figures in challenging poses.

BODIES AND ACTIONS

SOMETIMES IT'S REALLY hard working out how a character's arms and legs should go when you want them to do something specific like running, jumping, dancing or even just sitting. (Certain poses give me a real headache.) Never fear, Agent Beaker is on a mission to help!

Lightly sketch a stick figure with simple lines for the limbs. Try out a few doodles until you're satisfied with the action you're after – in this case a set of nifty ninja moves! Then you can work up the body shape, adding details to create a fully formed character.

How to draw . . .
TRACY BEAKER

Tracy Beaker needs no introduction!
She can be funny, feisty and ferocious,
but she's never boring!

Give Tracy lots
of springy curls

Tracy's got her hands on her hips
to make herself look important.

How to draw ...
BISCUITS

Biscuits appears in *Cliffhanger*, *Buried Alive* and *Best Friends*. He's great at baking.

Draw Biscuits' mouth quite high in his face to make his chin the right size

Perhaps you could design him a new jumper?

How to draw . . .
FABULOUS
FASHION

CLOTHES PLAY A huge part in the lives of Jacqueline's characters. Lots of them have very strong opinions about what they like and don't like to wear. Some of the girls go for pretty dresses and some of them prefer a tomboy look.

Try experimenting with spots, stripes and other patterns to liven up clothes in your pictures

FABULOUS FASHION

I spend a lot of time thinking about the right clothes for the adult characters too.

I based Jenna Williams' outfits on Jacqueline's own fabulous style!

These clothes were in fashion when Jacqueline was growing up

TRACY LIKES TO THINK her mum leads a glamorous life in Hollywood, wearing lots of designer frocks. Here are three outfits that might appeal to her.

Bouffant hair

Big earrings

Long gloves

Necklace

Boots

Fishtail

Ruffles

In *Little Darlings*, Destiny is determined to be a pop star. Maybe one of the looks opposite would work for her?

Cropped t-shirt

Flared trousers and trainers

One shoulder dress

Asymmetrical hem

Mini skirt

Ankle boots

Copy or trace this mannequin to design a glamorous costume for Tracy's mum, Destiny or yourself!

LOLA ROSE IS VERY impressed by her Auntie Barbara's cool accessories. Adding details like jewellery, belts and bags to your characters can make a lot of difference.

DIAMOND WEARS A pretty tiara
when she's performing. Have a go at
designing one yourself.

Start with an arc of pearls.

Position a few large gemstones.

Frame the stones with more pearls.

With straight, criss-crossing lines,
turn the stones into cut jewels.

Shade one or two
facets lighter than the
rest, and your jewels
will sparkle

Highlights add real shine

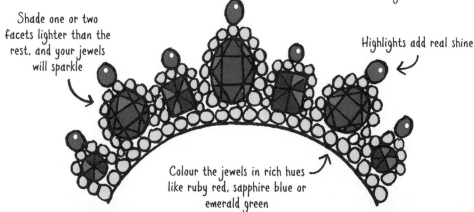

Colour the jewels in rich hues
like ruby red, sapphire blue or
emerald green

TINA'S GRAN IN *The Butterfly Club* is REALLY keen on shoes. Here are a selection for you to copy and practise.

Customize your own pair of trainers. Copy or trace the blank template and get creative!

Laces

Spots

Star

Velcro

Stripes

Zip

Ridged tread

WHAT WOULD YOU wear to a sleepover party - pyjamas, a long t-shirt or a nightie?

Here are some basic nightwear designs to copy and add patterns to.

Then there are lots of necklines to choose from.

Don't forget your slippers!

Here are some other things you might need for a successful sleepover . . .

How to draw . . .

MANDY AND TANYA

Mandy and Tanya appear in *Bad Girls*.
Mandy wishes she was allowed to wear
more grown-up clothes.

Tanya is a good friend to
Mandy, but her actions get
both of them into trouble.

Tanya likes
to wear eye
shadow . . .

. . . and very
high heels!

How to draw ...
WILLIAM AND CLAIRE

William and Claire are from *The Worry Website*. William is a sweet boy who could do with more self-confidence.

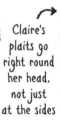

Claire's plaits go right round her head, not just at the sides

Claire's hobby is football and her hero is David Beckham.

How to draw ...

AMAZING ANIMALS

CATS AND DOGS PLAY an important role in Jacqueline's books. See if you can spot which stories these come from!

WOOF
WOOF
GRRR!!

In *The Cat Mummy*, Verity learns all about the Ancient Egyptians. This is the god Anubis who has the head of a jackal – a type of wild dog.

CATS ARE ONE OF JACQUELINE'S

favourite animals. They can be found in lots of her books like *Queenie* and *The Cat Mummy*. Here's how to draw one . . .

Start by drawing an oval in faint pencil.

Add triangles for the ears on top of the oval, pointing upwards.

Draw a rectangle for the body, making sure that one corner is hidden.

Add four legs and a tail.

Strengthen the outlines of your cat.

Now add the face and whiskers.

Now you've mastered the basic cat shape, experiment with putting the eyes and other facial features in different positions. You might be surprised at how different your cat starts to look!

Cats can be fluffy, stripy, or even floral!

Draw some extra details to keep your cat happy.

ALL HAYLEY WANTS in *Happy Holidays* is a dog of her own. Here's how to draw two different dogs: a little terrier, and a cheerful spaniel.

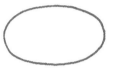

For both dogs, start with the simple body shape: a rectangle for the terrier, and a wide oval for the spaniel.

Then draw the legs. On the far side, these will be slightly hidden.

Then add the tail. Make it short and pointy for your terrier, and a curved, sausage shape for your spaniel.

AMAZING ANIMALS

Then add the head. Go for straight lines and sharp angles for the terrier, with pointy ears and a little beard, and curving lines for the spaniel, with floppy ears.

Strengthen the important lines, add the final details and colour in!

To suggest fur, use zigzagged or curvy lines.

Here are some ways to give your dog different expressions.

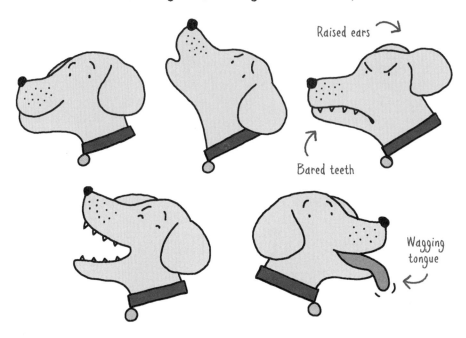

Raised ears

Bared teeth

Wagging tongue

How about drawing some accessories for pampering your pet?

AMAZING ANIMALS

I certainly got to draw lots of cats and dogs for *Paws and Whiskers*!

LOTS OF OTHER animals can be found in Jacqueline's books. Sometimes they're real, sometimes they're imagined and sometimes they're stuffed toys!

AMAZING ANIMALS

A TROUPE OF hardworking performing monkeys feature in *Diamond*, and rather more happily, Mandy has an impressive collection of toy ones in *Bad Girls*. Here's how to draw a cheeky monkey.

Begin with circular shapes for the head and tummy.

Add the limbs. Remember that monkeys have long toes!

Next come ears and the face.

You could go for a smile or a wide grin!

Radish is the name of Andy's tiny toy rabbit in *The Suitcase Kid*, and Lily is a floppy-eared real rabbit and TV star in *Cookie*. Draw your own bunny in four quick steps.

In *Glubbslyme*, Rebecca meets a magic, talking toad. Here's how to draw one - don't forget the warts!

IN *THE LONGEST WHALE SONG,*

Ella does a special project on whales and becomes quite an expert on them. My favourite kind of whale is a sperm whale.

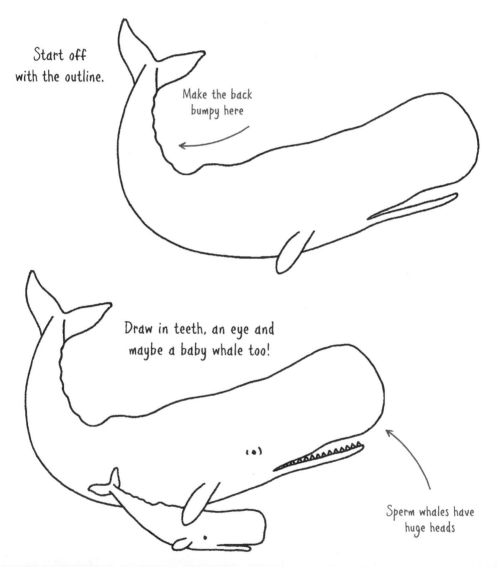

Start off with the outline.

Make the back bumpy here

Draw in teeth, an eye and maybe a baby whale too!

Sperm whales have huge heads

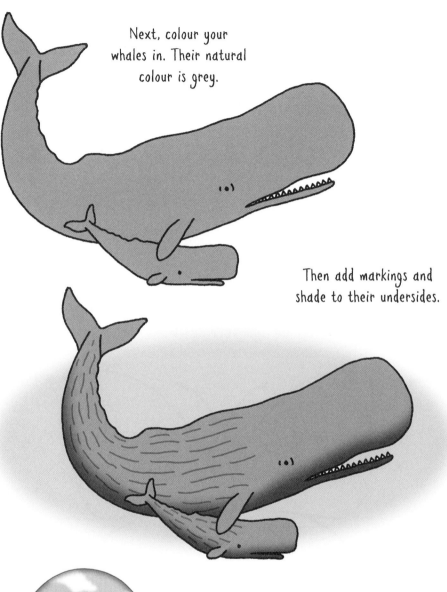

Next, colour your whales in. Their natural colour is grey.

Then add markings and shade to their undersides.

Ella is fascinated by humpback whales. They have knobs called tubercles on their heads and fins.

IN ***THE BUTTERFLY CLUB,*** Tina is obsessed with butterflies and with the help of her friend Selma, she creates a butterfly garden at her school.

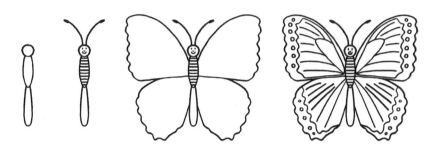

Butterflies are very simple to draw – but the markings on the left wings should be symmetrical with those on the right.

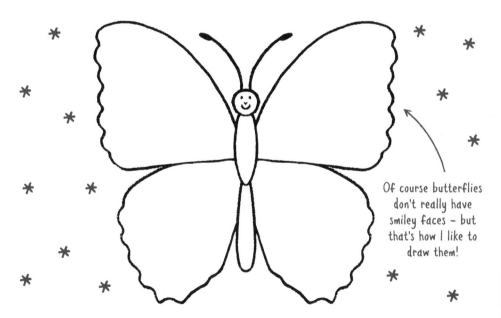

Of course butterflies don't really have smiley faces – but that's how I like to draw them!

Copy or trace this butterfly shape and add your own patterns to the body and wings.

IN *THE DINOSAUR'S PACKED LUNCH,*

Dinah visits a dinosaur exhibition at a museum on a school trip. She sees a tyrannosaurus rex and a triceratops, but likes the iguanodon, with its distinctive thumb spike, best.

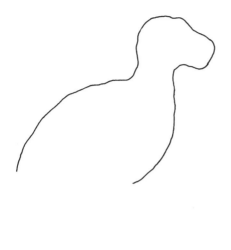

This is how to draw the iguanodon.
Draw lines for the body and head.

Add tree trunk-like legs and arms
with thumb claws.

Draw the huge tail, the eyes and
nostrils.

Nobody knows what colour dinosaurs were,
so you could make yours any shade you want!

HETTY FEATHER MEETS not one but two elephants in her first story. Here is the London Zoo elephant for you to copy.

Did you spot that this elephant has no tusks?

Jumbo, the famous elephant who lived at London Zoo in Victorian times, lost his in an accident, so mine doesn't have any either.

SEVERAL OF JACQUELINE'S

characters have imagined themselves or others as animals.

Have you ever noticed that pets and their owners can sometimes look alike? Have a go at creating people who resemble animals – it's easier if you start with a drawing of the animal first.

How to draw ...

HETTY FEATHER

FLAME-HAIRED HETTY is one of Jacqueline's most popular characters. She may be small, but she's very feisty!

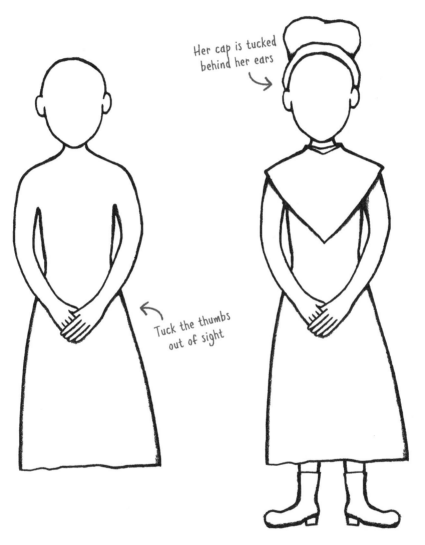

Her cap is tucked behind her ears

Tuck the thumbs out of sight

Start off by sketching the shape of her head, her skirt and her clasped hands.

Add Hetty's bib, cap, sleeves, and boots.

HETTY FEATHER

At the Foundling Hospital where she lives, Hetty has to wear the same scratchy uniform day in and day out. Here's how to draw her.

Have a look at page 31 for tips on how to draw plaits!

Draw in her face, hair, apron and laces.

Hetty's hair is a wonderful bright red and her dress is brown.

I **DECIDED TO** illustrate the *Hetty* books with silhouettes, as they always make me think of the Victorian era in which Hetty lived. I did a lot of research to make sure everything I drew looked right for the period.

It can be quite
effective to
pick out small
details in white

How to draw ...
PERFECT PARTIES

PARTIES – ESPECIALLY BIRTHDAY

parties – are often an important part of Jacqueline's stories, and they're always fun to draw.

PERFECT PARTIES

THE MORE DETAILS you add to a party picture, the more festive you make it. Here's a selection of useful party items.

A white highlight will make your balloons shine

You can't have a party without party food! What are your favourites?

Daisy's D.I.Y. pizza from *Sleepovers*

My favourite party food is the birthday cake. Lots of Jacqueline's characters have wonderful homemade cakes. In *Sleepovers* the members of the Alphabet Club munch their way through five particularly fine bakes!

HERE'S HOW TO draw a really special party cake.

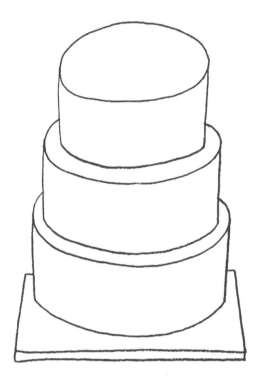

Start by drawing a tower made of three round cakes.

Decorate your cake however you fancy. You could put decorations or candles on the top, or . . .

... you could have someone bursting out of it!

Add a couple of sparklers and colour in delicious shades.

DOUBLE CREAM

PARTY CLOTHES ARE really great to draw. What would you wear to your dream party? Why not design your own outfit – here are some ideas to start you off!

Marty would be much happier in her favourite t-shirt and jeans!

Perhaps your dream party would be a Halloween party like the one Pearl and Jodie go to in *My Sister Jodie*. What spooky costume would you choose?

I **ENJOY DRESSING UP** for a fancy dress party and so does Tracy Beaker. Which of her outfits do you like best?

Trace this image of Tracy and add your costume ideas over the top!

ANOTHER TYPE OF party is a masked ball. These are elaborate parties where everyone comes wearing a different mask. Here are some ideas for designs.

Trace around the shape opposite, and perhaps draw in extra features.

Then cut out your mask, asking an adult for help if you need to. Attach a straw or lolly stick to the back so you can hold up the mask to your face. You might want to glue on beads, sequins or feathers.

You could ask your friends to make their own masks too, and throw your very own masked ball!

PERFECT PARTIES

SILHOUETTES CAN MAKE a great carnival parade! Start by drawing your characters in outline, then fill them in with a dark shade.

Now you're ready to add headdresses, wings and other striking decorative shapes. Guess who's leading the parade?

How to draw ...
LILY

Lily has a side parting and her hair hides one side of her face

Add darker brown pencil lines to Lily's light brown hair

In *Lily Alone*, Lily and her younger siblings are left to fend for themselves when their mum goes off on holiday.

How to draw ...
COOKIE

Draw her glasses first before sketching her eyes and eyebrows

Add a little shading to the hair below Cookie's jaw line

Beauty likes to bake biscuits - that's why her nickname is Cookie!

How to draw . . .
SEASONS AND
WEATHER

WHEN I'M WORKING on my illustrations, I always

consider what time of year it is in the story, so that I can draw the characters in appropriate clothing. I'll often put little details into the background, too, to indicate what the weather is like.

　　　　　　SEASONS AND WEATHER

SPRING

Spring can sometimes be a very rainy time. Don't forget to make your characters looks correspondingly soggy!

SUMMER

In summer the bright sun can cast strong shadows. It's time for sandals and sunglasses.

AUTUMN

WINTER

Nothing makes a picture more autumnal than leaves blowing in the wind. Scarves and hair get blown around too!

Snow will instantly make a scene look wintery. I find a tube of white gouache paint comes in handy for adding snow flakes.

HERE ARE ALL kinds of extra seasonal images from Jacqueline's books for inspiration.

SPRING

Be Mine

VALENTINE

SUMMER

AUTUMN

WINTER

HERE'S A REALLY easy way to give your artwork a foggy atmosphere.

Draw and colour your scene
in your usual way.

Place a slightly larger sheet of
tracing or greaseproof paper over
the top and stick into place.
Add an extra sheet for an even
foggier effect.

Clouds can be very useful for adding drama to a daytime or nighttime scene.

Two illustrations from Jacqueline's
Paws and Whiskers anthology.

If you're drawing a sunset,
make your clouds and sky pink.

Add shade to the bottoms of your rainclouds to give them substance.

The more you angle your rain, the more blustery you make your scene.

WHEN CHRISTMAS COMES

it's a lovely idea to make your own cards. Here's a suggestion for a reindeer card.

Draw the outline of the head and ears.

Add the antlers and a smiley face.

Pop some robins (or decorations) on the antlers.

Colour in festive shades.

Fill the empty spaces around your design with snowflakes, crackers, holly, Christmas puddings . . .

Here's an incredibly simple four step way to draw a snowflake. They always have six sides or points and no two flakes are ever the same.

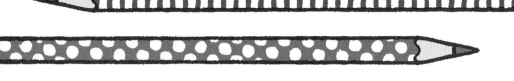

How to draw . . .
INSIDE AND
OUTSIDE

I'VE DRAWN LOTS OF different buildings in Jacqueline's books and all kinds of dwellings - from castles to caravans!

INSIDE AND OUTSIDE

The *Double Act* twins imagine living here one day!

Tracy's picture of her children's home

DRAWING A BUILDING at an angle will give it more realism. Have a go with Natalie's home in *The Monster Story-Teller*.

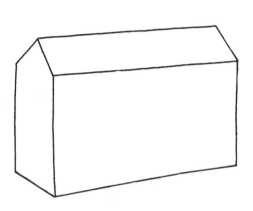

Draw the front and side first.

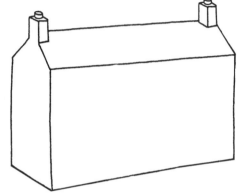

Add the roof and chimneys.

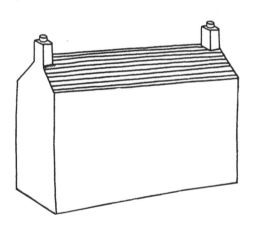

Put some tiles on the roof.

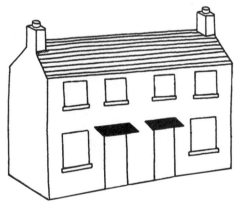

Add windows and doors.

Draw in the gardens and keep adding details.
I've put Natalie's mum and brothers sitting on their lawn.

WHEN IT COMES TO drawing interiors I think that the more details you can put in, the better. Including patterns will add lots of interest to your picture too.

INSIDE AND OUTSIDE

LOTS OF JACQUELINE'S

characters fantasise about the kind of homes they'd like to live in. Tracy would go for a bedroom like this.

Her friend Cam's flat is a bit untidy.

This is how Tracy would redesign it.

HERE IS AN empty room for you to trace or copy so you can design your own cool interiors.

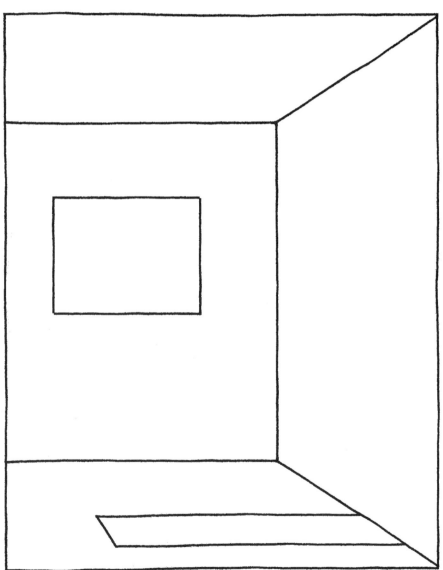

It's this way round! ↖

WHEN I'M DRAWING furniture and furnishings I often flick through magazines and catalogues for inspiration.

I **HAD TO RESEARCH** all kinds of Victorian household objects when I was illustrating the *Hetty Feather* books. Some things looked very different to their modern-day equivalents, and some things haven't changed at all.

Natalie's school in
The Monster Story-Teller

MOST OF JACQUELINE'S characters go to normal schools (one or two go to posh ones) but if they could, I bet they'd all like to go here!

Melchester College in
My Sister Jodie

ICE RINK

HELI-PAD

BOUTIQUE

DISCO

ACE H

One of the best things about drawing is that you can let your imagination run riot! What would your own dream school look like?

SHOPS FREQUENTLY feature

in Jacqueline's stories, like the boutique Indigo in *Bad Girls*.

Elsa and her mum have fun in a music store in *The Bed and Breakfast Star*.

NEW ALBUM

GREATEST HITS

In *The Monster Story-Teller* there's a pet shop selling monster pets!

Design a shop front for your favourite kind of store.
Here are four that I've created, but I've left the signs blank.
Can you think of a really good name for each shop?

Opal Plumstead would like this shop!

This shop is perfect for Tina's gran in *The Butterfly Club*.

How to draw . . .
JODIE

Her school tie is red and grey

You could colour in Jodie's earrings with a silver marker pen if you have one to hand

Jodie has red hair with gold streaks in *My Sister Jodie* – at least, she does to begin with! She also has lots of earrings.

How to draw ...
RUBY AND GARNET

Ruby

Garnet

In *Double Act*, Ruby and Garnet are identical twins, but Garnet is the quieter and neater of the two. To draw Ruby, make her hair a little untidy and her collar unbuttoned. (One shoe lace would probably be undone, too.)

How to draw . . .
GETTING
AROUND

IT'S AMAZING HOW many different forms of transport have cropped up in Jacqueline's books. You might be brilliant at drawing detailed cars and buses straight from memory, but I usually need some reference. Sometimes I use toy vehicles to help me!

GETTING AROUND

THIS IS TRACY'S picture of herself and her mum in a fancy sports car. Here's how to design Tracy an even snazzier automobile!

Start with an elongated shape like this.

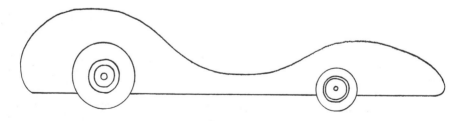

Add the wheels – the rear wheel can be larger.

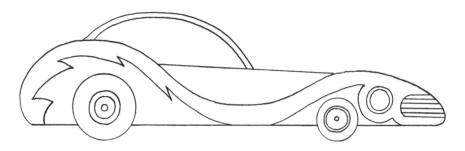

Draw the roof, radiator, and lights and add a pattern along the side panel.

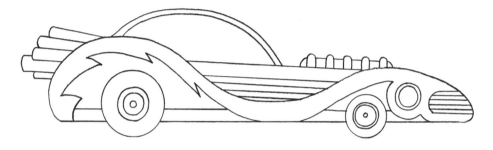

Don't forget the engine and the exhaust pipes!

Here are some essential items for Tracy to take on her journey.

TRACY MIGHT **WELL** imagine 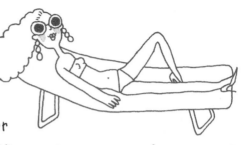 her mum relaxing on the sundeck of a huge cruise liner when she's off on her travels. Why not have a go at drawing one?

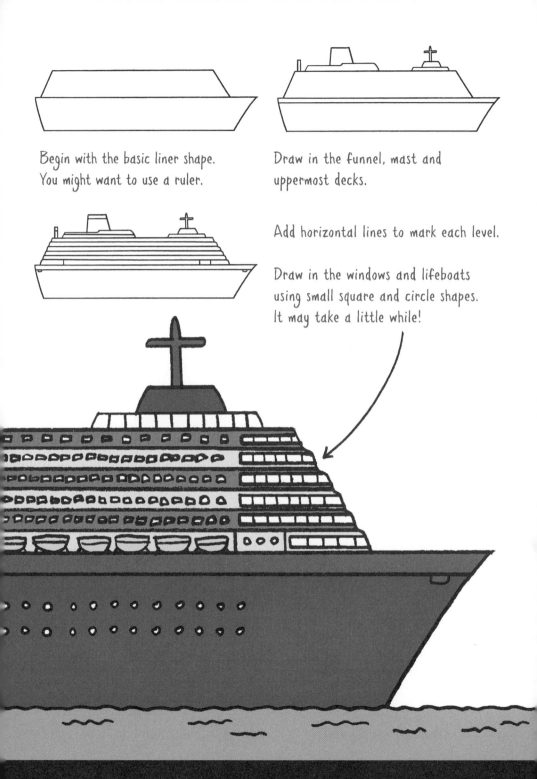

Begin with the basic liner shape. You might want to use a ruler.

Draw in the funnel, mast and uppermost decks.

Add horizontal lines to mark each level.

Draw in the windows and lifeboats using small square and circle shapes. It may take a little while!

IN ***THE BUTTERFLY CLUB,*** Maddie likes to make up adventure stories. Her favourite is about two children going up in a hot air balloon and landing in different countries. Here's how to draw one!

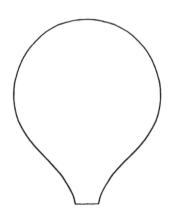

Draw the outline of the balloon.

Attach the basket.

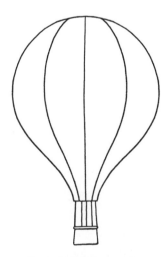

Give the balloon ribs.

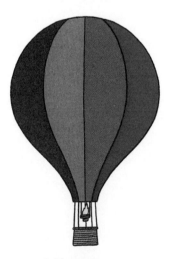

Add the burner.

You can make your balloon striped or decorate it with any patterns you fancy

Hot air balloons can come in all sorts of shapes!

How to draw ...
HOLIDAYS

WHO DOESN'T LIKE being on holiday – whether it's at the beach, in the countryside or somewhere abroad? Here are some items that might be good to include in your holiday pictures.

Jacqueline's characters go on all kinds of holidays and they sometimes send postcards.

Dear Gran and Grandad and Nibbles and Speedy and Cheesepuff

We are having a lovely time. Gran, please don't feed Nibbles too much as he's very greedy and can sometimes be sick. Especially don't feed him chocolates. Love Philippa

We have races on the beach and I always win! We go swimming every day. We even went in yesterday when it was raining. Love Madeleine

Mr and Mrs B. Maynard
42 Melrose Gardens
Wardle
Bishopsgrave
B1 2GT

I love love love it here.
Love Tina xxx

How not to Abseil

Help!

Me hanging by my fingertips!

A very long way down

Design your own postcard and write a message on the back. Tracy has included all the places she would love to go on her holiday.

105 mm

148 mm

This is the size of a real postcard, so trace around it or follow the measurements.

BEAKER TOURS

HERE ARE SOME holiday scenes from Jacqueline's books to inspire you.

I N *THE STORY OF TRACY BEAKER,* Tracy

draws a picture of her mum having a lovely time in Paris. Here's how to draw a slightly more detailed Eiffel Tower.

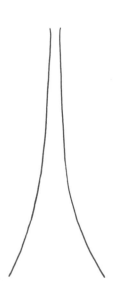

Start with two curving lines like this.

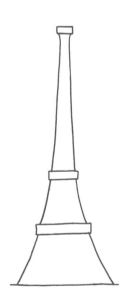

Draw the ground and the three levels.

Add more lines to create the legs, turret and arch.

Add a few clouds and birds to give a sense of height to your tower

Draw in the horizontal girders.

Carefully add the the diagonal supports. Take your time and be as neat as you can – it's worth it!

WOULD YOU LIKE to visit the pyramids in Egypt? Perhaps you're lucky enough to have been there already. In *The Cat Mummy* Verity learns all about the ancient Egyptians with her teacher Miss Smith.

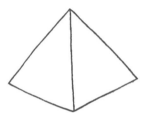 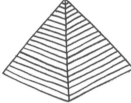 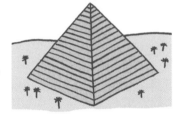

Drawing a pyramid is easy! Begin with two triangles. Next draw in lines for the steps. Then add a horizon and a scattering of palm trees.

Create your own Egyptian queen. Start with a head shape. Add a fine headdress with a serpent, hair and earrings. Finish off with a jewelled collar and exotic makeup.

Camels can be found in the deserts in Egypt. Here's a fun way to draw one.

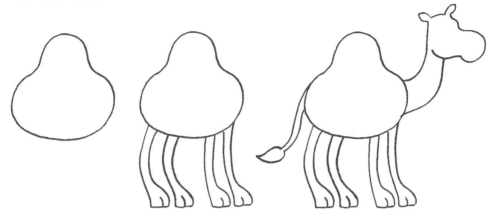

Draw a pear shape! Add in four legs, followed by a curved neck and the head. Finally give your camel a tail and facial features.

You might want to put some palm trees in the background to create a desert setting

IN *CANDYFLOSS,* Floss wouldn't mind a holiday in sunny Australia - but her mum and stepdad want to move there for six whole months!

Kangaroos have huge tails

Their back legs are big and strong

Here's how to draw Floss. Start with her head, curly hair and t-shirt. Add her arms and face. Draw in the finer details on her clothes.

Give her pale blonde hair and add a cool design to her t-shirt. I've chosen to add hearts and a koala.

A koala is really simple to draw. Start with an oval face shape, add the facial features and colour in!

How to draw . . .
MELISSA

Melissa and Marty are characters from *The Worst Thing About My Sister*. They may be related, but they're very different.

Melissa likes pussycats, perfume and pink! Once you've drawn her, surround her with girly accessories . . .

How to draw ...
MARTY

Marty is a tomboy and wouldn't be seen dead in pink! She prefers jeans, t-shirts and her favourite pair of tartan boots.

POW!

How to draw ...
MAGIC AND MONSTERS

JACQUELINE'S CHARACTERS ALWAYS

have vivid imaginations. They often daydream about possessing magical powers, or picture themselves and people they know in fairytale settings far removed from their real lives.

MAGIC AND MONSTERS

I got the chance to draw lots of fairy folk in *Midnight*, in which Violet loves the fantasy book illustrations of Casper Dream.

You'll notice that all these fantasy pictures are very detailed.
If you'd like to try one, go for a sharp pencil or a thin-tipped pen.

WHAT DO YOU think the most magical form of transportation is? How about a unicorn?

Bend the back legs forward a little

Start off by drawing a horse shape.

Add facial features, a mane, hooves and a tail.

Make these lines slightly wavy

Now turn your horse into a unicorn by adding a horn!

How about adding Princess Tracy?

Add lots of decoration to Tracy's costume and don't forget to draw in some reins.

Kiss me, Tracy – I'm secretly a prince!

In *The Worst Thing About My Sister* Marty has a fine collection of horses and ponies – but no unicorn!

TRACY ENJOYS DRAWING

herself as the naughty fairy Goblinda.
Have a go at inventing your own witches,
wizards, elves and fairies.

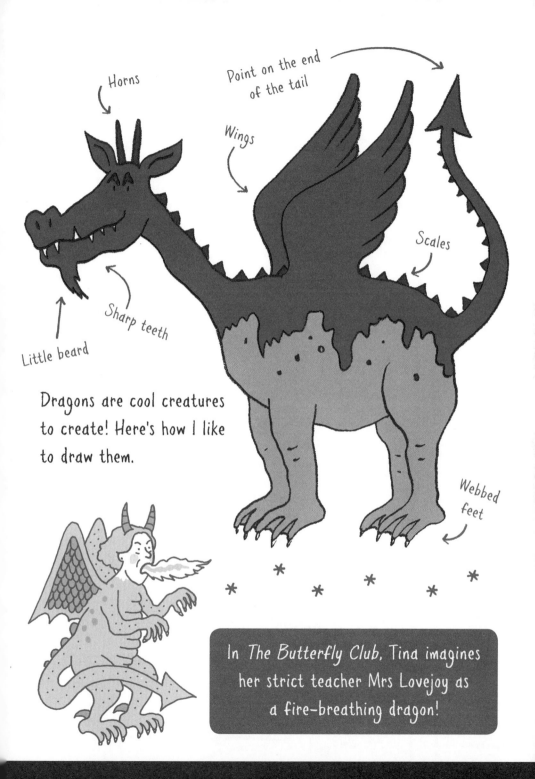

Horns

Point on the end
of the tail

Wings

Scales

Sharp teeth

Little beard

Dragons are cool creatures
to create! Here's how I like
to draw them.

Webbed
feet

In *The Butterfly Club*, Tina imagines
her strict teacher Mrs Lovejoy as
a fire-breathing dragon!

You might want to place your characters in a fantasy landscape.

When you colour in rainbows it's useful to remember the phrase 'Richard of York gave battle in vain' – red, orange, yellow, green, blue, indigo, violet!

MAGIC AND MONSTERS

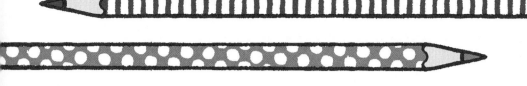

How to draw ...
SPACE

HAVE YOU EVER thought about what it would be like to fly off into outer space? Lots of Jacqueline's characters have and one of her books, *The Monster Story-Teller*, actually IS set on another planet!

TRACY IS ALWAYS ready for a new adventure - so how about space? Here's how to draw Tracy as an intrepid astronaut.

Start with a simple body shape. Make each limb quite wide - remember Tracy's wearing a spacesuit!

Add a perfect circle for Tracy's round helmet, with a screen for her to see out of, and boots and gloves.

For a fun shooting star, draw a basic star shape. Add lines coming from each tip that all meet up.

Inside the screen draw Tracy's face peeping out. Add all sorts of buttons, zips and patches.

Now add an oxygen pack and a tube to connect her to her spaceship. Give your picture a starry background – the more stars the better!

 To make a round planet look more three-dimensional add a moon-shaped shadow to the underside.

NOW TRY DRAWING Tracy in a spaceship so she can zoom off on lots of adventures!

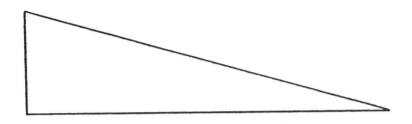

Start off with a long triangle shape. A ruler might be helpful here.

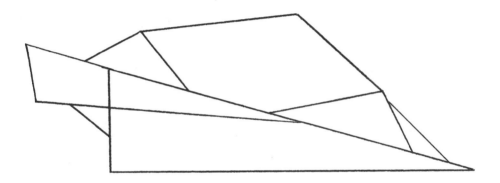

Add more lines to create a cockpit and a tail fin.

Alternatively you can create exciting forms of transport from a basic oval shape.

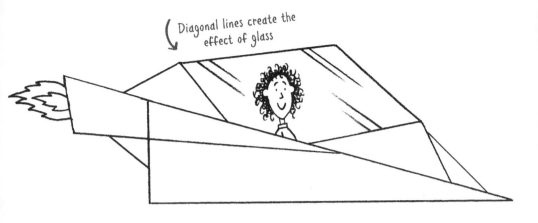

Diagonal lines create the effect of glass

Draw Tracy in the cockpit and add flames shooting out from the rear.

Add movement lines

Complete your amazing spacecraft by adding lights and dynamic graphic elements.

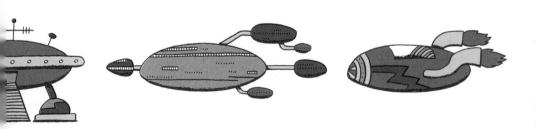

HOW ABOUT CREATING an entire space city? There are no rules about what shapes your buildings should be - in fact, the more bizarre the better!

Drawing small clouds in front of your buildings will make them look even more impressive

TRACY IS BOUND to meet a space monster on her journey across the universe. This is how she draws one herself in *The Story of Tracy Beaker*.

Inventing aliens is great fun. First, take any simple shape for the body. Circles, rectangles, triangles and ovals are all good.

Then choose what kind of legs, arms, eyes and ears you want to draw and how many of each! These elements might inspire you:

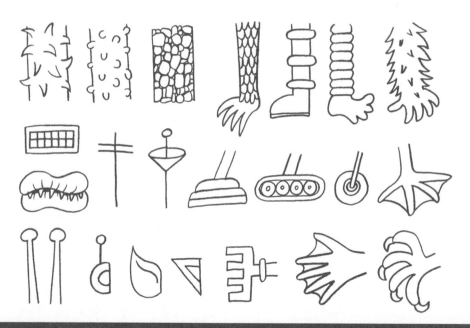

This alien seems quite friendly!

This one doesn't!

IN *THE MONSTER STORY-TELLER* Natalie

meets a monster from outer space who takes her for a ride on a flying saucer – a china saucer!

Here's how to draw Natalie and her funny friend.

Start off with Natalie's head and top half.

Continue with her bottom half and draw in her clothes, face and hair.

Now draw in the monster shape.

Add details to the monster
including his hair, face, claws
and a tail.

Now add colour. On the front
cover of the book I gave the
monster emerald green skin
and lime green hair!

How to draw . . .
YOUR OWN COVER

HAVE YOU HEARD OF the expression 'Never judge a book by its cover'? Well, I don't agree with that! I try to make Jacqueline's covers look as interesting and exciting as the story inside, and convey a little about the plot. At the same time I don't want to spoil things and give too much away!

Sometimes the title tells me immediately what I need to draw

It's important to make the title nice and clear

So that Jacqueline's name stands out really well
I almost always put it at the top

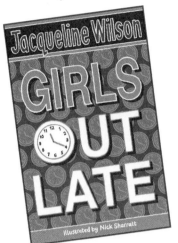

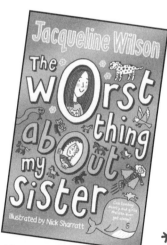

Letters can
become objects,
like this clock

I might place the title inside
part of the illustration

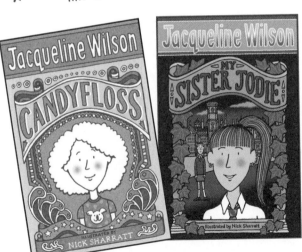

Decorative borders and frames can
make the design more attractive

Holes in letters can be
spaces for illustrations

***T**HE STORY OF TRACY BEAKER* has had a few different covers over the years. This design is very busy, with lots going on and the title as the main focus. Detailed covers give the reader plenty of things to look at and enjoy.

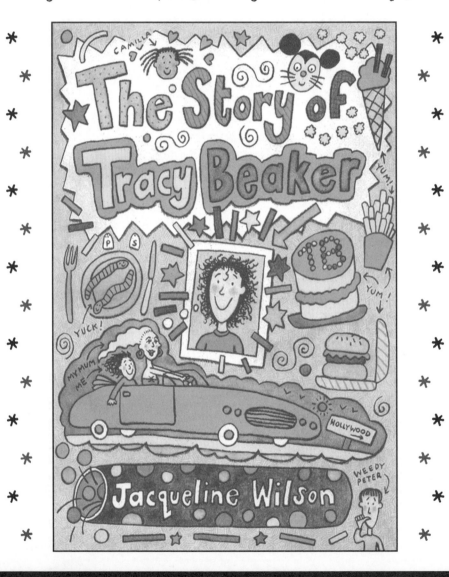

This cover is much simpler and the picture of Tracy is the focus. A large image of a human face with eyes that seem to be looking directly at you is a good way to attract attention, which is why magazines have faces on their covers so often.

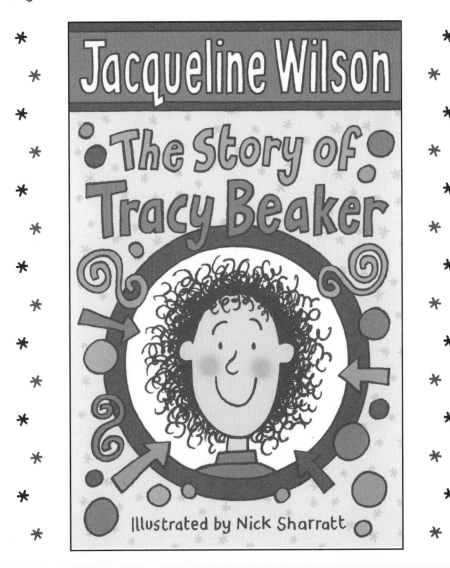

FOLLOW THIS EASY step-by-step guide to see how I often create the title lettering for Jacqueline's books.

I write out the title very lightly in pencil, leaving a generous space between each letter.

HOW TO DRAW

Then I draw around each letter.

HOW TO DRAW

Then I rub out the faint pencil lines.

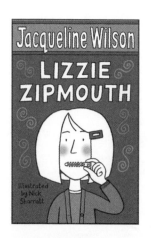

HOW TO DRAW

For a 3D effect I draw a little diagonal line from every corner. Then I link up the lines.

HOW TO DRAW

I colour the letter sides in a strong shade.

HOW TO DRAW

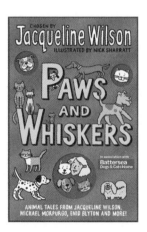

You could give your letters curves instead of sharp corners.

HOW TO DRAW

FOR MORE LETTERING ideas, take a look at the titles here . . .

Add pattern

sleep-overs

Vicky Angel

Cookie

Add illustrative elements

I made the lettering on the *Cookie* cover look like it had been written in icing to reflect Beauty's love of baking in the story

The Butterfly Club

Secrets

Lola Rose

Extra-large capitals

The Bed and Breakfast ✪ Star ✪

Joined-up lettering ↙

My Secret Diary

THE ⟨AT MUMMY

QUEENIE

OPAL PLUMSTEAD

LITTLE ♥ DARLINGS

↖ Old-fashioned lettering

All capitals ↙

★HETTY★ ★FEATHER★

CLIFFHANGER

The little lines that are sometimes added to letters are called serifs →

Add a drop shadow ↙

Double Act

Jacqueline Wilson

Copy or trace over the template on this page
and invent your own cover for your favourite
Jacqueline Wilson story.

YOU COULD DESIGN a back cover and write your own special blurb (a short description of the story). How about designing the spine too? Look at the cover I created for *Happy Holidays* for inspiration:

Spine

The writing on the spine faces this way

Front cover

Back cover

The illustration on the back cover and spine usually reflects the front cover design